I0829135

Proofs Considered

OF THE

Early Settlement of Acadie by the Dutch:

BEING AN

APPENDIX

TO

The Dutch in Maine.

On page 47 of **De Peyster's Dutch at the North Pole and Dutch in Maine**, the date of "1632" is set down as that of the first actual Dutch settlement in Maine. The authority referred to therein has never since been found, although diligently sought for by the writer on a subsequent visit to the coast of Acadie. (Me.) The death of "old settlers" and our people's carelessness with regard to papers are fast destroying evidences, of which former chroniclers availed themselves copiously. WILLIAMSON visited different localities, conversed with "old settlers," learned traditions, embodied verbal and written narratives, and thus compiled his valuable history. The nephew of that historian remarked in conversation, that SULLIVAN possessed himself of, and resorted liberally to sources of information no longer in existence when his uncle took up his pen.

Proofs, however, are by no means wanting, that the Dutch were in Maine prior to 1632.

Let us examine them in order:

The French claimed as far west as *Pemaquid* or Bristol, and the **Dutch** were continually interfering with their claims, and WINSLOW went to *England* to complain against both of those nations as early as 1635.

In 1607, GEORGE, brother of Lord JOHN POPHAM, Chief Justice of England, founded *Sagadahoc* colony, on the *Kennebec*. This failed, but WILLIAMSON records "that the coasts were never afterwards, for any considerable length of time, entirely deserted by Europeans, until the country became settled." (I. 203.)

HUBBARD'S New Ed. 37, says, "the *French* were here (1608) soon after POPHAM'S party left the place."—*Gorges' Hist.* 19,---5 *Purchas*, 1828,---*Princess' Ann*, 25. These references are from Williamson. (I. 203.)

And we know that the **Dutch** did not leave the *French* in quiet in these waters, for, in the same year, 1607, the French commandant, or governor, and council at *Port Royal*, now *Annapolis*, in *Nova Scotia*, received intelligence (WILLIAMSON, I., 204,) "by an early arrival in the spring (1607), of a transaction which proved *fatal* to the colony. This was an official report that the **Hollanders**, piloted by a treacherous Frenchman, had obtruded themselves into the Canada [i. e. Acadie or Maine] fur trade."

A *Frenchman*—highly distinguished for his virtues and accomplishments—the DUKE DE LA ROCHEFOUCAULT LIANCOURT, in the IId Volume of his *Travels*, at pages 465–'6, (4to, London, 1799) says: "Some attempts to settle a colony in this place, in the vicinity of *New Castle*, were made by the **Dutch** in 1625, and *even at the early period of* 1607, but without effect." Williamson (1.228. §) also refers to HUBBARD'S Narrative, p. 250, but the writer having examined all this author's works on New England, can find no mention of these events. Williamson, however, may have seen an original manuscript on this subject.

A Frenchman, in this regard, is a most reliable witness,

for he has no partialities of race or religion to gratify by conceding any achievement creditable to the Dutch. This renders their presence in Maine an absolute certainty, since all that was required was to substantiate the circumstantial evidence by the slightest reliable records.

These are the first *definite* announcements which are to be found at this day in print, of the arrival of the Dutch upon the coast of Maine.

CYRUS EATON, in his "Annals of the *Town of Warren*, with the Early History of *St. George's*, *Broad Bay*, and the neighboring settlements on the *Waldo Patent.* Hallowell, 1851, page 17–'8, ¶ 1623," &c. reads—

"Fishermen and settlers also established themselves about this time at *Sagadahoc*, *Merry-Meeting*, *Cape Newagin*, *Pemaquid*, and *St. George's*, as well as at *Damariscove* and other islands; though at *St. George's* it is believed there were not as yet any permanent residents. Adventurers from other nations also frequented the coast; and *it is said that the* Dutch, *as early as* 1607, *and again in* 1625, *attempted to settle at Damariscotta. Cellars and chimneys, apparently of great antiquity, have been found in the town of Newcastle;* and copper knives and spoons, of antique and singular fashion, are occasionally dug up with the *supposed* Indian skeletons, at the present day, indicating an early intercourse between the natives of the two continents. *Similar utensils, and the foundations of chimneys, now many feet under ground, have also been discovered on Monhegan, as well as on Carver's Island at the entrance of St. George's River*, where are said to be also the remains of a stone house."

Among the remarkable *Oyster Banks*, on both sides of the *Damariscotta River*, (according to E. ROLLINS and M. DAVIS,) cited by WILLIAMSON, [I., 56—Text and Note,*] "skeletons and bones of human beings are found," "yet no tradition about them has come to the present generation."

All this goes t orender the French Duke's remarks a certainty.

Let us examine these matters in order:

First, when the English made their first settlement at *Pemaquid* or *Bristol*, which was planted before that at *Boston*, (SULLIVAN, p. 164,) in 1623–'24, they found vestiges of a previous attempt at colonization, which, taking everything into account, points to the **Dutch** as their authors. Wherever they settled, their first labor was, if practicable, the construction of canals and the assimilation of their new homes to the dear ones they had left in the Low Countries. Even in *Java*, at the risk of introducing, in their company, the deadly jungle fevers, they intersected their infant metropolis with canals.

Grant that this is in a measure conjectural; EATON's investigations alone (without what has gone before and without de la Rochefoucault Liancourt's assurances, transmute it almost into a certainty.

"The earliest settlements seem to have been on the western banks of the *Pemaquid River*, in 1623 or '4. * * * A fort was built there, the year before the date of the patent, and rifled by pirates in November, 1632. Formal possession was given and taken under the same instrument, May 27, 1633. * * * * The visitants, as well as inhabitants, were highly pleased with the situation of *Pemaquid*. A smooth river, navigable a league and a half above the point, a commodious haven for ships, and an eligible site for a fortress, at once filled the eye. Here was a canal cut 10 feet in width, and variously deep from 6 to 10 feet, on the east side of the river which passes the first ripples."—("It was 20 rods in length; and passed down a smooth inclined plain [plane]. No water runs there at present.")—"an enterprise devised and finished, at a time and by hands unknown." (WILLIAMSON, I., 242.)

"Below the Fort" (*Frederic* or *William Henry*, previously *Fort George*,) "was a handsomely paved street, extending towards it, northwestwardly from the water, 60 rods. It is still to be seen; and like the canal, it is the work of *unknown* hands." (WILLIAMSON, I., 57.)

Patient investigation of all the concurrent circumstances, and cool reflection, lead the writer to assign these labors to the **Dutch**.

"The History of *Georgetown*,"—(originally situated on both sides of the river, but now divided thereby into *Georgetown* and *Bath*)—is "the history," says SULLIVAN, page 169, "of the river *Kennebec*."

On an island, already spoken of, called *Stage Island*, was the landing place of POPHAM's party, in 1607. Governor WINTHROP says they came in 1609. OGILBY, in his collection, which he made in the year 1671, says, that they landed on the west side of the river, on a peninsula, and there began a plantation. HUBBARD—(whose book is very rare and costly)—says, that a party came from England, and settled at *Kennebec*, in the year 1619. Soon after POPHAM's party left the river, *in* 1608, *the French took possession of it.* In the year 1613, Sir SAMUEL ARGALL went from *Virginia* and removed them. *On the island are the remains of a fort, several wells of water, and several cellars; the remains also of brick chimneys have been found there, and it is very clear that the bricks which were used in the buildings must have been brought from Europe.* On the west side of the river are the remains of a fort, made of stone and earth: there are also eight old walls now to be seen, and the ruins of several houses. *Whether these buildings were erected by the English, or by the*

French, is uncertain; but the probability is, that the former were the erectors of the works." (SULLIVAN, pages 169–170.)

"*Stage Island*, in the District of Maine, lies south of *Parker's* and *Arrowsike* islands, on the North side of *Small Point*, consisting of 8 acres, not capable of much improvement; and is only *remarkable for being the first land inhabited in New England, by a civilized people.* It is not *now* inhabited." (MORSE'S *American Gazetteer, Boston*, 1797.)

Why should it be more probable that the *English* were the architects than that the **Dutch** were the fabricators? It is well known that the **Dutch**, in this country, were large importers of brick for building purposes, and may have ballasted therewith vessels fitted out for discovery. SULLIVAN tells us, in a note, at page 170, that he saw these remains, causing the ground to be opened, in 1778." *Now, had the bricks been English, he could have easily recognized them by comparison.* The *French* resorted to the materials at hand for their constructions; whereas the **Dutch**—besides coming from a land destitute of stone—were exceedingly partial to brick, and *their own* brick. All these things considered, the probabilities are far greater in favor of the **Dutch** than of any other people.

Second, *Carver's Island*, near the west bank of the mouth of *St. George's River*—which flows up to famous *lime-producing Thomaston*—offers for the investigation of the antiquarian some very interesting remains. There are said to be the appearances of a very ancient settlement. *Monhegan* or *Manhegin*, at the extreme western mouth of *Penobscot Bay*, has also unexplained vestiges of former occupancy. This was, without exception, two hundred and sixty years ago, the most famous island on the seaboard of Maine. "The island of *Matinicus* was inhabited very early, and "remains of stone houses are still apparent, generally supposed to have been built by French or **Dutch** fishermen," "though unknown." (WILLIAMSON, I., 63–'4.)

Finally, to sum up, consider the "Appointment of the installation of **Cornelis Steenwyck**, and the fact that the **Dutch**, according to SULLIVAN'S own admission, in 1673 or '4, expelled the French and made themselves masters of that very country, which comprehended all the settlements to which we have alluded. The same author admits that the French claimed to the *Pemaquid*, and all historians concede that they claimed between 40 deg. and 46 deg. of northern latitude, and exercised jurisdiction over the whole country generally known as *Acadie* or Maine. What took the **Dutch** there? They were not given to poaching upon other men's manors, but were fiercely tenacious of their own, and vindicated their rights at times, with a determination which bordered, though rarely, on ferocity. But had they not suffered too deeply from the Spaniards, and other would-be oppressors, to be called upon to suffer any longer willingly? The English, on the other hand, were apt disciples of that School which taught "conveying" into their own pockets, ship's holds and jurisdiction, any lands, &c., in the power of nations too weak or too sluggish to resist their encroachments. If the **Dutch** did settle the coast of Maine, 1607 to 1632, and were driven thence either by famine, the natives, the English, or the French, they had a right to seek to establish themselves in their ancient possessions, so hardly won. What was good to be taken, was also good to be retaken. This was sound English doctrine, and had a royal authority in GEORGE II., in his letter of advice to the Empress MARIA THERESA, with regard to the aggressions of FREDERIC the Great. The writer feels assured, not only that the **Dutch** were the original settlers at different points of the coast of Maine, but also indulges his suspicions that the early Massachusetts and Anglo-Maine people knew the facts, had the proofs, and suppressed them. English historians' very avoidance of the subject, their vague intimations and "probabilities," all tend to instill such an idea. To admit the claims of the **Dutch** as the original colonists, was to invalidate their own. May the documents yet be found substantiating that *Acadie* was **Dutch** before an English eye looked upon her evergreen forests, or pressed her mossy shores!

The subsequent connection of the **Dutch** with Maine has been narrated at length in the "Paper," read 3d March, 1857, before the **New York Historical Society**.

At page 50—reference is made to the settlement of New Plymouth.

Knikkerbakkers should never forget that the PURITAN colonists came from **Holland** and intended to settle upon the **Hudson**. They having made a mistake in the quality of the territory where they located themselves, charged the fault upon the Dutch, whom they accused of bribing their Captain to misdirect them. Of this they had no proof, and we have just as much right to believe that they sought the shores of Acadie, having heard of the availabilities of the Kennebec and Penobscot as well as of the Hudson, for the Dutch had actually attempted to settle between the first two rivers before they discovered the third.

At page 56—reference is had to the cession or grant of a district of Maine to the Duke of York, afterwards James II. By this, in 1664, the County of New Castle in Maine became appendant to his Province of New York, and his governors and agents were invested with jurisdiction over the territory between the St. Croix and the Kennebec, as well as the **Dutch** settlements on the Hudson and Delaware.

EATON, Pages 21--'2, reads with regard thereto:

"The Duke caused a city named Jamestown, and fort,

called fort Charles, to be built at Pemaquid,and many Dutch families to be transported thither from New York. Considerable uneasiness was occasioned to these eastern settlements by the war declared by France in 1666, and by the recession of Acadia to France by the treaty of peace in 1667. However disagreeable, the French were allowed to take possession as far as the Penobscot; but on their demanding the rest of the Province as far as Sagadahoc, the people of Pemaquid and vicinity, averse to the jurisdiction of France, preferred coming under that of Massachusetts."

This averseness is by no means to be wondered at when we recollect what sufferings the Dutch protestants at home had suffered at the hands of the Romanists, who, whether Spanish or French, were equally inimical to those of the *truly* reformed Saxon Evangelical Church.

"After this pacification" of 1688,resumes Eaton,(26)"till the abdication of James IId, the arbitrary conduct of the agents sent by his deputy at New York for the management of affairs here, gave little encouragement for the re-settlement of the country; but many **Dutch** families were induced to settle at Pemaquid and on the west bank of the Damariscotta, *who*, at the latter place, then called New Dartmouth, now Newcastle, *entered upon the business of agriculture with such spirit and success as to gain for the settlement the name of* "THE GARDEN OF THE EAST." In 1688 Sir Edmund Andros made two expeditions to this quarter, in the first of which he attempted to take possession of the country east of the Penobscot, but contented himself with plundering the Baron de Castine of his goods, furniture and ammunition. This affair irritating the Baron, led the tribe, over which his influence extended, to unite with the Abenaques in a second Indian war, which in August, of that year, was begun by an attack on N. Yarmouth. In September, New Dartmouth was burnt, and the inhabitants, with the exception of two families taken prisoners, saved themselves only by taking refuge in the fort. At the same time the fort and buildings at Sheepscot were also destroyed and the settlements entirely broken up. The **Dutch** settlers, discouraged, left the country; and both places, so lately and so long inhabited and flourishing, lay waste about thirty years."

At page 47, **D. in M**, mention is made of a subsequent accession of German settlements at Broad Bay. A great many Germans were induced to remove thither and to the parts conterminous by General SAMUEL WALDO, many of whom in 1750 established themselves on what was then, and is still, known as **Dutch Neck**. The original **Dutch** colonists, of whom but few survived the intemperateness of the climate, the assaults of the priest-instigated Indians, and the other manifold vicissitudes of an exposed north-eastern frontier life, were soon lost sight of among the more numerous Germans or High Dutch who were induced to take up their abode on the Waldo patent; yet, notwithstanding, they made an indelible and honorable mark on the history and upon the map of Maine.

Some farther interesting matter with regard to the **Hollanders**, in our most eastern state, *may* be found in the "Papers relating to **Pemaquid** and parts adjacent in the present state of Maine, known as Cornwall county when under the colony of New York, Compiled from Official Records in the office of the Secretary of State at Albany, N. Y., by Franklin B. Hough, 1851," and the "Ancient Pemaquid, an historical review, prepared at the request of the Maine Historical Society for its Collections, by J. Wingate Thornton," both published in the Vth volume of the Collections of the Maine Historical Society ; funds having been provided by the Legislature of that state to transcribe and print the same.

But, besides these, there is still a vast amount of manuscripts to be examined at Albany, which should throw a flood of light upon this interesting subject. The following, an extract from a letter of HENRY ONDERDONK, Jr.,Esq., of Jamaica, Long Island, is too important not to be made public.

"Hardly one in a thousand would have dreamed that the Dutch ever had any thing to do with Maine. My attention was called to it by two documents relating to the claims of **Denis Hegenan** (Hegeman ? a Knickerbocker name) for injuries sustained during his mission to *Pemaquid*. This was some years ago, and I had to enquire where Pemaquid was, and wondered what in the world the Dutch had to do there. I found one of the papers in the U. S. Collection of our Colonial Documents in the State Library at Albany, at the end, or nearly so, of Vol. 47. (There is no Index.) "Lucretia Heyenan, widow of Denis, petitions Governor and Council for relief. Her husband was sent by Gov. SLOUGHTER with letters to confer with the Indians at Pemaquid, who had sided with the French in the war of 1691. He reached *Penobsquid* and was persuaded by the French to come on shore, when he was seized and sent to Canada and kept a prisoner there 2 years, then sent to France. So that it was 3 years and 3 months before he returned home. £50 was paid her.

Vol. 39 has a petition from Denys Heyenan himself (1694) in which he states his wife is a Prisoner in Canada.

Vol. 45 has affidavit of **Jno. Cornelisse** who was deck hand on board the vessel that took Heyenan to Pemaquid. Vol. 47 has affidavit of **Daniel Remsen** to same effect. The The names are all **Dutch**.

I have abridged the above very much, but could (write) them (out) more at length if they were of any use. The originals are more full than the abstract I made.

Perhaps the preceding refer to too late a period for your purpose. It is the winding up of the Dutch Colony I should think."

It would seem from all these that the **Dutch** who were even at that time experiencing so much injustice and persecution at the hands of the French in Holland, were not to be exempt, in a measure, from the same suffering in their new homes on this continent, and that the ocean was to prove no barrier to the woes which the ruthless hand of war made so fearful wherever the industrious and the enterprising sought, however distant, to worship, cultivate and dwell in peace.

At home about this time horrors were multiplied.

Between **Woerden** and **Leyden**, on the Old Rhine, in Noord Holland, the road passes the beautiful villages of *Zwammerdam* and *Bodegrave*, together with the first city, so fearfully "memorable as the scenes of the atrocities committed by the

French army, under Marshal Luxemburg, in 1672. Their cruelty, as described by Voltaire, is not exaggerated: so great was the hatred which it inspired in the minds of the Dutch who were witnesses of their conduct, that descriptions of the war, called "Fransche Tijrannije," were written and printed as school-books for their children to read, calculated to hand down an inheritance of hate for their enemies to future generations."

EUGENE SUE, in his "Histoire de la Marine Française" (II. 286–'7), Frenchman as he is, cannot resist transcribing from the "Annales des Provinces Unies" the account of these monstrous horrors, the natural and inevitable consequences of the invasion of Holland by Louis XIV.

☟ ☟ ☟ ☟ ☟ ☟ ☟ ☟ ☟ ☟

"The two villages of Zwammerdam and Bodegrave, comprising six hundred dwellings, were reduced to ashes; but one remained, which escaped by accident the fury of the soldiers and the general conflagration. The destruction of the heretics churches was made a religious duty; not one was spared. The public buildings where justice was administered experienced the same fate. The soldiers who had conceived this cruel design issued forth from Utrecht armed with matches and other combustible materials. They shut up the father and mother with their children in their own home in order to destroy a whole family at one blow, and when the ashes and ruins of the houses were removed a quantity of half consumed corpses were discovered, as well as infants burnt in the arms of those who had given them life. A mother whom decrepid old age had rendered blind, and an object worthy of compassion, was murdered in the presence of four children who supported her, and had, with them, one tomb amid the flames which reduced them all to ashes. As if cruelty was diversified to the utmost, another matron who had reared an equal number of children beheld them murdered before her eyes, and was then immolated herself by the fury of the butchers. The Prince of Orange, who arrived two days afterwards in these places, found a number of children whose arms and legs had been cut off, and other mutilated bodies, which he left a short time without burial, and exposed to the eyes of those who passed, that they might learn from this frightful spectacle what they might expect from the (Roman Catholic*) French. The soldiers diverted themselves by seizing these innocent creatures by the feet, tossing them into the air and catching them upon the points of their pikes and swords, happy thus to die since some were afterwards precipitated into the flames, and new torments were devised to deprive the others of life. They violated daughters in the presence of their mothers; wives under the eyes of their husbands; and the (French) soldiers who could not find a sufficient number of objects to gratify their brutality, because they were too numerous, satisfied in turn their infamous passion on one and the same person, even to the number of twenty and upwards, and then spared such the misery of surviving their shame by casting them into the water and the fire. Avarice joined to cruelty animated the officer as well as the soldier. They (the R. C. officers and soldiers) suspended men in the chimneys of their houses and kindled therein great fires in order that suffocated and burnt, in turn, by the smoke of the turf and the flames which burst forth afterwards, they might be compelled to discover the money they possessed, and often which they did not possess; to such a degree were they (the French) victims of an imagination equally sordid and barbarous.

Ordinary executions and cruelties not sufficing to glut the fury of the soldiery, they (the French) invented extraordinary ones. They stripped the young girls and women whom they had violated, and chased them entirely naked into the open country, where they perished with cold. ☞A SWISS officer finding two girls, of a respectable family, in this state, gave them his cloak and some linen which he had, and, proceeding to his post, recommended them to a FRENCH officer, who, very far from protecting them, having abused them in the (open) street, abandoned them afterwards to the lust of his soldiers, who, after having outraged them to the utmost, cut off their breasts, larded (pierced) them with the ramrods

*Explanations in (—), asterisks and capitals inserted by translator.

of their muskets and left their bodies exposed on the levee which leads from Bodegrave to Woerden. ☞ They cut off the breasts of other women, whose wounds they afterwards sprinkled with pepper, salt, sometimes even gun powder to which they set fire, to make them die more cruelly. One of these wretches who, at Bodegrave, had the barbarity to cut off the breasts of a woman in the act of lying in, and to put pepper thereupon, died in the hospital of Nimwegen in a frightful state of despair of a frenzy caused by the violent remorse of an outraged conscience, which presented continually to his mind the image of this female, whose agonized cries he imagined he still heard. They attached others by the hair or under the arm pits to trees in order that they might remain exposed in a disgraceful nudity to all the inclemencies of the atmosphere. A boatman was nailed by the hand to the mast of his vessel and his wife violated before his eyes, while he was forbidden to turn them for a moment from so infamous a spectacle, under pain of death. Many other husbands experienced the same fate, and were compelled by blows of the cudgel or the flat of the sword to be eye witnesses of similar outrages. In fine they did not even respect the bodies of the dead. Two corpses on their way to burial were stripped of the shrouds which covered them; the one was thrown into the fire with its winding sheet, the other was dragged out of it and had the water of the canal for a sepulchre.

* * * * * *

Eugene Sue then enters upon an indignant review of these infernal outrages.

"Let us recall—the writer has endeavored to translate literally—that long chain of villainies, of crimes, of sacrilegious venality, of perjuries, of corruptions, which connects those two years, 1670 and 1672; from that infamous treaty concluded in the midst of peace against the Seven Provinces to the devastation of that unhappy Republic; from the prostitution of Mademoiselle de Keroualle to the new treason of Louis XIV. towards England; to the massacre of the brothers de Witte.

* * * * * *

"But that which perhaps is still more frightful, or that which in truth calls forth a smile at its air, sufficiently Homeric, is to see that from the great poet even to the grave historian, that from the prince of the church even to the vicar of Jesus Christ (the Pope), each wished to pay, upon his knees, his cowardly tribute of ignoble flatteries, of shameless and wicked praises, with regard to this frightful invasion, its disgraceful causes and sacrileges and its sanguinary results."

"Thus the severe Boileau, the great satirist, the pitiless censor, in his cold and base declamation, not content with shouting "*glory to Louis!*" grows audaciously merry again at the uncouthness of the names of "*those smoking ruins subjected by the incomparable conqueror.*" He finds nothing but silly pleasantries, unworthy of even a college pedant, in connection with those unhappy, pillaged, devastated cities, which could only extinguish the flames which devoured them by engulfing themselves beneath the waters of the sea."

* * * * * *

"Then, after the satirist, comes the grand tragedian, the historiographer of France, the tender and religious Racine. A person should read his "Precis de la Guerre de 1672" to be able to believe; to remain confounded at the tone of placid, ingenuous simplicity with which he exposes the griefs of the "great king" against that little republic, "*whom her riches and abundance rendered formidable to her neighbors.*" "

Listen to him:

"This little republic monopolized the commerce of the East Indies, where she had almost entirely destroyed the power of the Portuguese. She treated on equal terms with England, over whom she had gained glorious advantages, and whose ships of war she had recently burned in the Thames; and at last blinded by prosperity she commenced to despise the hand which had so often established and sustained her. She pretended to give the law to Europe, she leagued herself with the enemies of France *and boasted that she alone had set bounds to the conquests of the king*—(always that folly about the medal of Joshua). She oppressed the Roman Catholics" (what a falsehood of Holland, of all countries ever the most tolerant) "in all countries of her dominion, and opposed the French commerce in the Indies. In a word she forgot nothing which could draw down upon her the storm which was about to overwhelm her.—The King, tired of suffering *her insolences*, declared war against the Hollanders early in the spring and marched against them."

"Then after many assertions as singular as the foregoing: *Never did a prince* (Louis XIV.) *keep his word so religiously.—It is a matter scarcely susceptible of belief that in the fidelity which he* (Louis XIV) *maintained towards his allies, he always evinced greater anxiety for* (took greater care of) *their interests than for his own.*"

* * * * * *

"But this is not all," resumes Sue, "after the poets with their pagan allegories, after the fulsome Olympian adulations should succeed (in order) the servile Christian flatteries. After thundering Jove, after the ancient Rhine surprised among the timorous water nymphs amid his green rushes we have" (according to these exalted sycophants) "Jehovah crowning with victory the work so amorously well commenced by Mademoiselle de Keronalle; we have the god of armies mightily aiding Louvois to sadly embarass Colbert."

"In a word it is no longer Racine, Boileau, Bossuet, those elevated master spirits of reason and intelligence, who exalt and consecrate in marvelous language the most disgraceful carnal appetites, the most horrible perjuries, the most ferocious and impious enterprises; it is now that personage, who, according to the hierarchy of the (Romanist) christian world, is just inferior to God but superior to kings, the most imposing personification of human virtues, he, who throned upon the summit of the social edifice, alone receives from God the devine and solemn mission of representing him upon earth in all his majestic purity; it is he who can bind and loose here below; it is the Pope, in a word Pope Clement X, who writes with his pontificial hand the following brief to Louis XIV, who was then resting from his conquests in the beautiful arms of Madame de Montespan, after having just exiled her inconvenient and sorrowful husband."

"To our dear son in Jesus Christ apostolic greeting and benediction!

"The universe contemplating the overthrow by your victorious arms of a power raised upon the ruins of a legitimate authority, and otherwise injurious to the interests of royalty, felicitates Your Majesty, whose youthful brow is decorated with glorious triumphs and adorned with magnificent spoils. The bowels of our pontificial charity cannot longer restrain themselves, and we behold with a joy equal to your own the augmentation of true religion combined with the success of Your Majesty, a joy which corresponds with the grandeur of those powers with which the divine goodness has invested us. In effect the churches restored to the (Roman) Catholics, the religious discipline re-established in the cloisters, the priests fulfilling the divers functions of divine worship, the inhabitants enabled to practice the truth without restraint; such are the results which suffice to prove that Your Majesty's mission is from on high, since it thus advances with the stride of a giant in the path of victory.

"Permit then, most Christian King, in order to consolidate the glorious results already obtained both by war and by peace, our zeal and our apostolic affection to excite even yet more your royal piety, that, thus, you may better be led to understand upon several points our nuncio, the archbishop of Florence.

"Meanwhile we will not neglect to lay at the foot of the throne of divine mercy the paternal sentiments with which our heart is filled for your preservation, and the success of our prayers for the glory of God to the end that the apostolic benediction, which we bestow upon you, may derive its confirmation and strength from that propitious source.

"Given at Rome, at St. Mary the Greater, under the seal of the fishermen, the 23d August, 1672, the IIId year of our pontificate.

Archives of foreign affairs, Rome, 1672,--Supplement.

Let the foregoing speak for themselves. Contrast the atrocities in Holland sanctioned by the "most christian king," for had he not endorsed them he would not have justified the subsequent devastation of the Palatinate, the persecution of the Protestants; the dragooning of his Reformed subjects; the revocation of the Edict of Nantes; the breaking on the wheel, the burning, the racking of evangelical pastors for teaching God's word in all simplicity—and the judgments which followed. Starvation, ruin, misery, invasion, humiliation, gathered like avenging furies about the last days of this "most christian king." The Almighty answered the prayers of the Romanist vice-god with curses instead of blessings. Defeat and disaster crowned the "great king" with ashes instead of laurels. The tomb closed upon the magnificent Sultan of France amid the execrations of his own people, and jests not sighs, congratulations not tears, trooped along side the funeral procession which conducted the remains of the greatest egotist in history to the resting place of his ancestors. That prince of Orange whose temporary defeat moved "the bowels of pontificial charity" lived to move those same bowels with a lively sympathy in his own behalf for the humiliation of that "most christian king" whose christianity was the christianity of despotic self-exaltation. The armies of protestant Holland and England trampled under foot those blood stained banners which had floated so triumphantly over the ruins, the ashes, the violations, the murders, the tortures, the sacrileges of their defenders, and France drank blood enough within the next century and a half to quench the most raging appetite for slaughter. The congratulations of Pope Clement X. were echoed by the execrations of Pope Pius VII.; the rejoicings of the restored Romanist priests of Holland were echoed by the wails of the priests of France beneath the axe of the guillotine, the sabre, the pike, the bayonet of their fellow citizens. The smoke of the Dutch villages was answered with an hundred fold density by the steam of the slaughter pits of France, and if such are the responses which await the papal henedictions far be those benedictions from us and ours. Clement blessed Louis XIV. and his royal sun stooped, paled and set in gloom. Childless, he closed his eyes in the full light of Holland's triumph and England's glory. His great grandson and successor died a loathsome object, deserted, despairing, corruption itself even before the grave exerted its sovereignty. And that great grandson's successor and grandson swallowed the very dregs of the cup of humiliation, and then poured forth his life upon the scaffold, and his poor boy perished, when, how we know not, an object of compassion to all who hear his pitiable story, by a fate which wrenches the heart of every father who has read the narrative.

Well might my ancestor's kinsman—writing from Holland, 22d July, 1707, a few years after the horrors of the French invasion, when the ebbing tide had borne back to France the miseries it had borne on thence so proudly with its flood, but while the storm was yet abroad npon the continent, ejaculate, "We earnestly hope that God may soon exempt us from this ruinous warfare, and graciously grant us a lasting peace; but above all peace, that liberty of conscience which, in value, far exceeds all human powers of estimate."

(Johan de Peyster, in Rotterdam, to Johan de Peyster, in New York.)

Martyrs of Holland, in the old and new world, vengeance was with the Lord so impiously invoked to sanction your sufferings, and he repaid and will repay to the uttermost.

But, alas! man in all ages seems—without the *real* influences of *true* religious training and discipline—to be, and have been, the same untamed, ferocious animal. Christianity, at all periods, has found some strongholds impregnable even to its appeals, even in the midst of communities possessing the highest development of secular civilization.

A few days since has taught the world that education and the influences which are supposed to render men gentle, could not restrain an American community from imitating, or a county from applauding, conduct which—in the writer's opinion—would disgrace the most barbarous-unconverted or fanatical-converted horde of the most excitable race.

Rose Hill,

Tivoli, Dutchess Co., S. N. Y.

23d September, 1858.

www.ingramcontent.com/pod-product-compliance
Lightning Source LLC
LaVergne TN
LVHW011146110826
845150LV00008B/2546
9781418191795